WILD FRUIT

WILD FRUIT
by
SNOWDON

Text by Penny David
Foreword by Sir David Attenborough

BLOOMSBURY

To David, Sarah and Frances

First published in Great Britain 1997
Bloomsbury Publishing Plc, 38 Soho Square, London W1V 5DF

Text copyright © 1997 by Penny David
Photographs copyright © 1997 by Snowdon

The moral right of the author has been asserted

Designed by Price Watkins

A CIP catalogue record for this book is available from the British Library

ISBN 0 7475 3700 3

10 9 8 7 6 5 4 3 2 1

Printed in Singapore by Tien Wah Press

FOREWORD

by Sir David Attenborough

Fruits are supposed to look nice. Cezanne certainly thought apples did. Lots of Dutch painters, a couple of centuries earlier, felt the same way about grapes. And who can resist a ripe, shiny, black-as-jet blackberry in a hedgerow?

One cannot say, of course, that fruit evolved to please the human eye. Strawberries and apples, grapes and figs were producing their fruits long before human beings appeared on this planet. Their delectable colours and tastes developed to tempt not human beings but birds and mammals who, having eaten them, would carry away the pips, stones, pits – the seeds – in their stomachs and ultimately deposit them far away in a place where a seedling would not compete with its parent. For my part, I find it delightful rather than not to think that I share some aesthetic tastes with blackbirds and finches and monkeys.

But even more pleasing to me are the seeds themselves, particularly when they are carried unadorned on stems. They have no need to look seductively pretty, for they rely for their transport either on the wind, or on hooks and barbs which will attach them to fur or feathers. They are hard and uncompromising. Often they manifest that elemental geometry that is the basis of so much of the universe, and can be seen in crystals as well as in the flowers from which seeds develop – three-fold, four-fold, five-fold. But they fascinate me most of all because they have an ability that humanity yearns for but has never yet possessed – and may never do so. Most seeds, under the right conditions, will remain viable for centuries. A magnolia seed excavated in a prehistoric village in Japan germinated after a wait of two thousand years. Lupin seeds that fell into crevices in the ground during the Ice Age, when mammoths trod around them, have remained frozen, but alive, for at least eight thousand years.

The strange and beautiful objects portrayed in the following pages, whether plumed with crests of hair, equipped with propellers, embedded in sweet flesh or armoured and unadorned, are all travellers – not just in space, but in time.

1997

WILD FRUIT

OLD MAN'S BEARD

*As the year matures to December dotage, hoary greyness coats
the roadsides in limestone and chalk country. The long, long shoots
of clematis, whose leafy tendrils elbowed up and over hedges and
into trees, froth with fluffy seed-heads that catch the waning light.*

*Fruit? Yes – or rather, a veritable cornucopia of fruits.
Each unobtrusive flower has become a spiralling mass of cobwebby
filaments. Each single strand consists of a seed – an achene –
attached to an elongated wispy style. The plumes catch the wind so
the feather-light seed can be borne great distances. The old man
has a twinkle in his eye: his rampant beard assures fecundity as his
progeny go forth and multiply. It's also called Traveller's Joy.*

MEDLAR

'You'l be rotten ere you bee halfe ripe, and that's the right
vertue of the Medler.' Shakespeare was right: it takes a frost to
'blet' the raw fruit until it is half-rotten and edible.
(In warmer countries you can pick ripe fruit off the tree.) The taste
of the soft, slightly granular flesh is compared to baked apple
or 'winy custard' – good raw with a sharp cheese,
or whisky or port, or cooked into compotes and fruit butters.

The medlar's fruits look like rounded brown rose-hips
(it's a relative of the rose). The flower leaves behind five persistent
sepals, between which you glimpse the seed chambers
inside: with typical robustness, Elizabethans called these 'open-arse'.

STRAWBERRY

Someone quoted in Walton's Compleat Angler *says:*
'Doubtless God could have made a better berry, but doubtless
he never did.' Since then Man has bred them ever bigger
and brighter, but the little wild strawberries remain sweetest of all.
Botanical boffins tell us the strawberry is technically not
a 'true fruit' at all, but an enlarged, red, fleshy receptacle, full of
juicy pulp: the actual fruits are the little pips (seed-like achenes)
dotted over the surface. But as we pop the sweet morsels
into the fleshy receptacles in our faces and savour the juicy pulp,
do we care? Not a straw.

GUELDER ROSE

It is, of course, not a rose at all but a viburnum, and related to
honeysuckle and elder. This native ancestor of the cultivated
snowball tree borrowed its name in the sixteenth century from
shrubs seen growing in Gelderland in eastern Holland.
(The flat white flower-clusters look a lot more like snowballs
than roses.) The astringent, waxy berries suggest
the American name of European cranberry bush. It is decorative
in both spring and autumn. Gertude Jekyll described its
habit as 'a stiff-wooded thing, the character of its main stems
being a kind of stark uprightness'. She supplemented
its 'great white balls' of flowers with starry garlands of
Clematis montana.

WOOD MUSHROOM

No one could understand how mushrooms grew without a root;
they must be 'earthie excrescences', engendered by thunder.
'They come up so hastily, as in a night, and yet they are unsown,'
Bacon marvelled. Even when the invention of the microscope
showed minute, seed-like spores, some doubt remained about the
nature of the beast: one Münchhausen in the eighteenth century
thought spores were the eggs of small animals who lived
in the fungus. Gradually the mysteries were unravelled to reveal
a vast network of invisible underground threads that periodically
produces fruit-bodies. Yet still most species of mushroom
defy domestication: they just grow, like Topsy.

ELDER

Plump black berries, heavy with juice and the power to do you good.
Raw, they're purgative: concoct them into wine or cordial
for them to work other magic. John Evelyn praised the 'incomparable
spirit' made of the berries, and his contemporaries preferred
the spiced drink ebulum to port for its 'pleasant taste and healthy
quality'. Winemakers took to using elderberries to supplement
the grape harvest in bad years (Portugal actually banned elder
cultivation). Cheaper, elder-adulterated port was effective against
rheumatic aches and pains.

Pick flowers for fritters, sorbets and lotions; pick leaves to deter flies;
but think twice before cutting (let alone burning) the wood.
Or at least, ask the tree spirit's permission before you do.

HAZEL

Wisdom in a nutshell. First the nut forms from the female flower,
fertilized by airborne pollen from a dangling male catkin
(each lamb's-tail bears some four million pollen grains). Then an
animal agent carries it off to a cache somewhere and forgetfully
lets it germinate. The finest resulting plants, bearing cobs
and filberts, were long ago selected by breeders as the ones to
cultivate for fruit. The trees were coppiced for hurdles,
house-building and a hundred other things. In the wild, however,
the hazel could become as rare as the elm:
greedy grey squirrels harvest unripe nuts, thwarting regeneration.

SEA BUCKTHORN

*Bright orange berries of female plants make food for birds
as well as an astringent sauce or jelly. (Remember the 'sea' part
of the name: don't try the shiny black fruits of the
plain buckthorn, which have spectacular purgative properties.)*

*A silvery-grey scaly coating on the leaves enables this shrub
to endure seaspray and salt winds, and it is planted to stabilize
coastal sand dunes as well as to decorate city streets,
where winter gritting makes life salty. In its element, along
sea-coasts, this buckthorn spreads both by seed and by suckering
roots, creating impenetrable spiny thickets of monoculture
that exclude companion plants, fixing fragile sandscapes at
the expense of wider floral diversity.*

LORDS AND LADIES

*The knobbly nakedness of the wild arum's fruits
has prompted scores of suggestive nicknames, from 'dog's dick' to
'cuckoo pint' (rhyme with 'hint': it's short for pintle, or penis).
Girls were warned not to touch it for fear of pregnancy.
Little wonder the plant was considered an aphrodisiac. John Lyly had
it in mind when he wrote in* Loves Metamorphosis *(1601): 'They
have eaten so much of wake robin, that they cannot sleep for love.'*

*The plant has other, more practical properties that impart stiffness.
In Gerard's day the roots were used to make 'the most pure
and white starch' for laundering ruffs, though the acrid juices of this
starchwort were 'most hurtfull' to the poor laundrymaids' hands.*

ASPARAGUS

The berries that stud stray female plants at the end of summer are not what Gerard had in mind when he commended asparagus's capacity for 'increasing seed...'. These hapless fruits produce unwanted offspring, and gardeners do away with them (pigeons fancy them and thus spread some seed). It is, appropriately, male plants that are prized in beds for the way their shoots spring forth plentifully. People from Pliny to Madame de Pompadour shared Gerard's earthy view that asparagus was good for '...stirring up lust'. It seems to be the phallic appearance of the thrusty young spears that excited all these ideas – enhanced later, perhaps, by the relish involved in eating the succulent morsels.

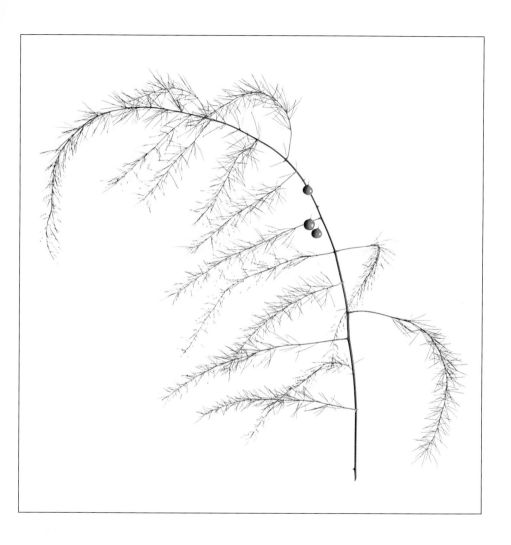

STRAWBERRY TREE

'She may very well pass for a strawberry/
In the dusk with a light behind her!' (pace Gilbert and Sullivan) –
if you were dim enough to go berrying up a forty-foot arbutus tree.
The warty, globose fruits ripen to red (but take a year to do so,
and taste pretty dull: the Latin unedo means 'I eat just one!'): you
find them in late summer along with next year's panicles
of white urn-shaped flowers amid glossy leaves. One of the few
members of the heather family to grow to tree size, Arbutus unedo
is native in Atlantic Spain and Portugal as well as the west
of Ireland – a once-continuous population split by the last Ice Age.

LABURNUM

*Dangling yellow pea-flowers (also known as golden chain)
are followed by pods of seeds where the deadly alkaloid
cytisine carried in all parts of the tree – roots, wood and bark –
becomes concentrated. Next to the yew, the laburnum
must be Britain's most poisonous tree. People get ill after carrying
twigs or flower sprays in their mouths, and carthorses tethered in
the shade of a tree died after eating pods and leaves.
Yet the laburnum is popular as an ornamental (a laburnum
'tunnel' is the June glory of many a garden), and upland farms in
western Britain include mile upon mile of old-established
laburnum hedging. Did those canny farmers risk poisoning stock
to harvest the ebony-like timber, or for the transient pleasure
of lining their fields with gold?*

OAK

*The majestic oak can support a staggering amount of wildlife,
from tortrix moths and toadstools to tree-protesters.
Five hundred kinds of invertebrate munch their way through
various parts of the tree and its heart-of-oak thrives on the
attention. Even the fruit is not immune. A newcomer arrived on
the scene in the swinging sixties: the acorn cup gall wasp,
Andricus quercuscalicis ('just call me Andy'). The host tree reacts
to his or her presence (gall-wasp sexuality is a confused business)
by enveloping the new-laid egg with a layer of tissue, effectively
sealing it off from the main part of the plant.
The greenish sticky excrescence of this knopper gall provides
board and lodging for the developing larva.*

CHINESE LANTERN

Just as the spud is a versatile veg, with starring roles
(from Mash to Mr Chips), its relations are masters of disguise.
The simple, creamy-white flowers of this potato-cousin
give way to conspicuously ornamental fruits. The persistent papery
calyx inspires the title (though sometimes the lantern is Japanese).
Scrutiny reveals the lamp's fivefold veined segments
that correspond to each flower's five lobes.

A more prosaic image underlies the botanical Physalis,
from the Greek for bladder (hence bladder cherry).
Indeed, we have ransacked the fruit-bowl (and the atlas) to find
names for kindred species. More succulent and tasty berries,
though in less flamboyant casings, include Cape Gooseberry,
Strawberry Tomato and Cossack Pineapple.

MISTLETOE

*A Christmas peck beneath the mistletoe is a faint echo of potent
fertility rites. Pliny, who advocated a drink of berries to cure
barrenness, described Druidical dealings with mistletoe on oak (lopping
it off with a golden sickle in ritual emasculation). Centuries
of superstition followed, fuelled by the plant's mysterious parasitic
growth and somewhat wanton look.*

*Mistletoe has a suitably ambiguous sex-life. Male and female plants
are needed for fruiting. Fertilized females develop berries; though
single-seeded, they are polyembryonic and can produce several seedlings.
What looks like a single plant may be a congregation of both sexes.*

*Pliny thought mistletoe sprouted only when defecated by a bird;
we know you can glue the seed you plucked after your Christmas kiss
to your chosen tree – but wait till spring for best results.*

SLOE

*Blackthorns are abundant in hedges, and sloes are prolific
on blackthorns. The dusky bloom-coated drupes cluster
on the spine-defended twigs well into winter. The meanest and
bitterest of the stone fruits of the plum family, sloes are
nevertheless too plentiful to waste. Pick them after a frost, prick
the flesh, add sugar and top up with gin. Strain off the liquid
to drink after three months or so. An alternative sloe-and-sure way
of laying your neighbours low is to use the dense timber of the
blackthorn in time-honoured fashion to make that 'Irish
tranquillizer', a shillelagh.*

ROWAN

*Mountain ash is another name: the pinnate leaves
superficially look like those of ash, and it is a true mountaineer,
growing at higher altitude than other trees in Britain.
The fruits are equally tenacious, hanging on while other berries
drop to provide winter food for the birds that disperse the seeds.
Their taste is bitter, though they can be cooked to serve with game,
made into ale and wine, and even (in Scotland, naturally)
distilled. Rowan's specific name,* Sorbus aucuparia, *derives from
the Latin* auceps, *or 'bird-catcher'. Hungry
people used rowan berries to attract and trap small birds.*

HOP

Closely related to cannabis, the hop has similarly narcotic properties. Lupulin, the resinous substance tucked into each of the fruit's scaly bracts, provides the bitter principle that gives beer its astringent taste and its keeping qualities. (An alternative way to sedation is to sleep on a hop-filled pillow.) In Tudor England Continental-style beer made with hops began to challenge traditional sweet malted ale, prompting Andrew Boorde to express some misgivings: '...it doth make a man fat and doth inflate the belly'. It's the females that are to blame: only they produce the cone-like inflorescences, and a hopfield is an all-female stronghold.

QUAKING GRASS

Dithery dock, doddering dickies, jiggle-joggle, wiggle-woggle, totty grass – who'd have thought a mere grass would set in motion such a welter of nomenclature? It's also called Quakers, like the Society of Friends bade by George Fox to 'Tremble at the Word of the Lord', and Shakers, like Ann Lee's jittery breakaway sect who left to live in temperance, celibacy and America.

Back at the grassroots, flower arrangers quiver with pleasure at the idea of including the graceful spikelets in a display. The superstitious get agitated about bringing the unlucky plant indoors – unless they're plagued by mice, which are supposed to dislike its smell.

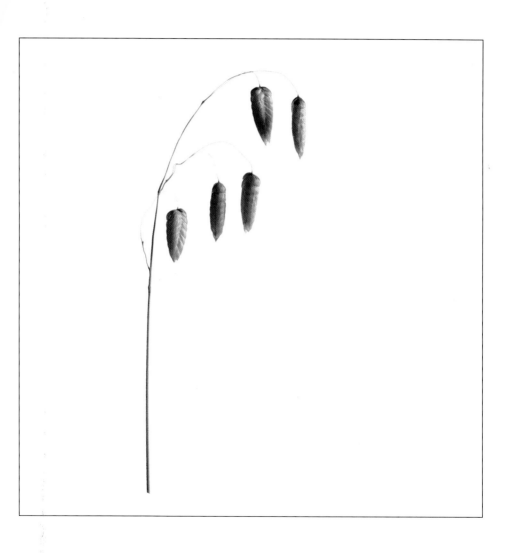

SWEET CHESTNUT

Clusters of seeds with shrivelled styles still attached
to their tips nestle in silk-lined protection. Sharp spines radiate
in clusters on their fearsome hedgehog armour,
defying soft-mouthed, soft-handed animals from interfering
with the unripe fruit before they have a chance of falling
on to soft earth and germinating. Chestnuts and their like rely
on gravity and animals for dispersal: in this nut-case they
engaged the might of the Roman Empire. They were introduced to
Britain nearly two thousand years ago and have successfully
naturalized. The strain the Romans brought does not bear nuts
as plump and floury as those around the Mediterranean,
but small is beautiful, and ours are sweet chestnuts.

SPINDLE

*Shocking-pink capsules shaped like cardinals' birettas
(or, for more prosaic Protestants, like pincushions) eventually burst
to reveal sticky orange seeds that dangle from their casing.
When the leaves take on autumn tints the colour palette is gaudy
indeed. Besides providing yellow dye for butter and a handy
purgative, these 'louseberries' were dried and ground as a treatment
for parasites of the genus Pediculus, or headlice.
The spindle tree was also planted near homes for its fine-grained
yellowish wood. This was burnt to make charcoal for drawing
and gunpowder. Or it was turned into knitting needles, skewers,
violin bows, virginal keys – and spindles.*

TOMATO

The tomato has had a rollercoaster ride since it hitched a lift
across the Atlantic with the conquistadores. The golden apple or
pomo d'oro – *the first ones were yellow* – was regarded
with suspicion as potentially poisonous, or at least aphrodisiac.
Gardeners grew them as decorative curiosities (as they did
scarlet runner beans). Gradually more palatable red tomatoes came
in to infiltrate the hearts and sauce bottles of the world.
Today their seeds germinate in garden compost heaps, while
waste-disposal operatives find fields of them sprouting in sewage
slurry. Flushed with success, these fruits have achieved a new
world-wide distribution via a super-efficient dispersal mechanism,
by passing through the human digestive tract intact.

BLACKENING WAXCAP

They bejewel the autumn grassland with their glowing colours –
ruby, amber, jade, ivory (even ebony). You find them on old,
moss-mellowed lawns and in ancient pastures unspoilt by
'improving' man. They are indeed precious, like the wild orchids
that thrive in the same places, indicators of a vanishing,
vulnerable habitat so easily destroyed by a sprinkling of fertilizer,
weedkiller or well-intentioned ignorance. They are called waxcaps
because they do indeed look and feel waxy-smooth and shiny.
Before it aged to don its silky widow's weeds, this specimen gloried
in a bright scarlet-orange cap and gleaming yellow stem.

WESTERN HEMLOCK

How familiar are you with the way mice smell?
(With their noses, yes); but did you know it resembles the weed
hemlock – Socrates' poison and the container Prometheus
used when he smuggled fire to earth? Encountering some trees with
what they considered a similarly mousy smell, early settlers
in the American colonies named them hemlocks. (Never mind that
the poisonous plant they remembered from back home was
a parsley relative and the new one a towering conifer.)
Later, in the 1850s, plant collector John Jeffrey discovered its
cousin in the Pacific northwest, hence 'western hemlock'.
Officially, botanists use the Japanese name, Tsuga.

Norway Maple

The maples multiply on a wing and a seed.
Fertilized flowers turn into two-part fruits in which each seed wall
stretches out sideways to form a delicately veined wing.
When the seed is mature and dry this papery membrane catches
the wind and allows potential progeny to be carried some
distance from the parent plant. Nicknames for these whirling seed
capsules are helicopters, or locks and keys, or hooks and hatchets.
The technical term for this arrangement is the glamorous-sounding
samara: in fact, a double samara. Except that surprisingly often
individual fruits have three or even four divisions, making them
triple- or quadruple-seeded.

GOOSEBERRY

You could almost chart the decline and droop of a nation's morals in a profile of this fruit. The phrase 'playing gooseberry' – acting as chaperon – is first recorded in the year Victoria ('I will be good') came to the throne; a century later, curious children were fobbed off with the idea that babies were found 'under goosegog bushes'. Meanwhile the industrious artisan was having a ball breeding the native berry: by Victoria's jubilee nearly two hundred Gooseberry Clubs were exhibiting ever bigger and better specimens out of some two thousand named varieties. Today few people know (let alone grow) the worthy fruit: fashion, food fads and moral fibre itself have made ours a post-gooseberry phase.

DAMSON

*The damson is the Damask Plum, with firm flesh that
needs cooking to release the rich flavour and juices. Its ancestor
came from Damascus long ago (archaeologists find the stones
in digs in Europe and Asia Minor). Famous old varieties
with names like 'Black Prince' and 'Blue Violet' still survive in
corners of England, but the varying fruits of country hedges
are the progeny of anonymous wild plums and bullaces that have
hybridized randomly over centuries. Before food was imported
and chemical dyes invented, huge quantities were harvested for
preserves and for the cloth industry. No fancy damask here:
just workaday wools and cottons.*

MULBERRY

*'Observe the mulberry tree,' advised John Evelyn; once it unfolds
its leaves you can be sure frosts are over and it's safe
to move your tender plants outdoors. His was the mulberry's heyday:
two generations earlier James I, attempting to set up an English
silk industry, had ordered the planting of masses of mulberries and
published a monograph on the subject. The silkworms demurred,
disliking the climate, but the mulberry had arrived.
Trees have remained an ingredient of good gardens, and one or two
venerable Jacobean originals are still around.*

*In World War II Mulberry meant D-Day and Normandy.
Today D-Day is when you go round and round your mulberry bush
and Delicious fruits Drop in your Dish.*

OPIUM POPPY

*The biology of the poppy-fruit does not rely on providing
a flashy, flavoursome food-source for animals: the tiny seeds show-
er forth freely from pepperpot holes once the dried capsule
is shaken by wind. Plants are widely cultivated for the high-quality
oil in the seeds. In warmer climates the unripe seed-heads
yield a precious milky sap which becomes opium, with vast powers
to soothe and to enslave. The alkaloid principle morphine is named
after Morpheus, god of dreams (codeine comes from the Greek
name for poppy-head). The precious, pernicious plant has thus
spread itself around the globe by intricate distribution mechanisms
– thanks to human carriers and their capacity for pain, poetry
and poppycock.*

S NOWBERRY

*This straggly, suckering shrub of hedgerow and woodland
is part of our Victorian legacy. Huntin' and shootin' squires planted
it on their estates as cover and food for their game birds,
along with rhododendrons and other aliens. The berries still provide
late winter food for blackbirds, and bees enjoy the flowers.
Overall the plant is undistinguished, but it's worth taking a
magnifying glass to the marble-sized berry. As in so many plant
parts – flower petals, for instance – the quality of whiteness
is a matter of texture. People describe the snowberry as pearly, waxy,
even lardy. The spongy berries contain light-refracting air-spaces,
like icy crystals in snow – so the name is especially apt.*

SCOTS PINE

*It begins in spring. Male cones issue clouds of pollen
(mostly wasted on the wind). Young females, soft and reddish-purple,
open slightly to receive a share, then close up again,
sealing their scales with pitch. Eventually fertilization takes place
within. The cone grows to woody hardness until, two years later,
its dry scales open to release winged seeds. These naturalize
in southern Britain, or are planted. They are famous as waymarkers
along old tracks; groups of pines marked places where travellers
could find hospitality. But the old pine forests that once blanketed
Scotland have been scotched over the centuries – for timber,
charcoal, turpentine, tar; by deer, sheep and Sassenachs.*

WILD SERVICE

The roots of this tree, etymologically speaking, are far removed from everyday connotations of service. They are nothing to do with serfs and servants (Latin root servire*), but come from the old English name* syrfe*, which in Latin is* Sorbus*. Should you want to serve service berries, however, make sure they are overripe by hanging them up to 'blet', like medlars.*
Their pedigree as edible fruits stretches back to Neolithic times.
The Romans pickled the berries or preserved them in alcohol (still a good idea). Apicius gives a recipe for an egg-thickened dish called a 'patina', cooked in a kind of Roman bath or bain-marie*, and consisting of service berries and brains.*

CHILLI PEPPER

*Chilli seeds germinate readily in spring and plants will fruit
in the summer sun. Cooks discard the seeds under
the misapprehension that this reduces the fieriness, but it's in the
pithy membrane that the alkaloid capsaicin is most concentrated.
Eating chillies is good for you: capsaicin is antiseptic,
stimulates the gut, improves the circulation and does all sorts
of wonderful things. It also makes you feel good by triggering
the release of endorphins, the body's natural painkillers.
Handling chillies is less fun: minute quantities harboured under
fingernails or on kitchen implements can irritate sensitive skin
hours later. No wonder tormentors have used it to perfect
exquisite tortures.*

IVY

The plant has a dual personality.
In its youth, clad in typically lobed ivy-leaves, it wanders around
carpeting the ground or becomes a determined climber, using
its adventitious roots to cling to minute fissures in the surface of
a support. Once it reaches the top of its tree it changes character,
producing adult leaves of rhombic shape, fertile shoots
without the fringing rootlets, and flowers. Cuttings taken from this
part of the plant themselves turn into bushes rather than climbers.
Ivy is valuable to wildlife as cover and food; ripe fruits feed
blackbirds but could make a child very ill. And the weight of an
over-vigorous ivy can bring down an already-sickly tree.

HENRY'S HONEYSUCKLE

*This handsome black-berried climber, a modest cousin
of our more come-hither honeysuckles, was brought back from
China by the intrepid plant-hunter E. H. Wilson.
He named it after Augustine Henry, an Irish doctor who worked
for the Chinese Imperial Customs service, and who helped
Wilson locate the desirable handkerchief tree or Davidia on his
first Chinese expedition. It was Henry who, by alerting British
botanists of potential plant losses in the widespread destruction of
forests in China, spurred many great plant discoveries around
the turn of the century. These were no tranquil willow-pattern
scenes: when searching for the regal lily, Wilson broke his leg
in an avalanche and afterwards bore what he called his 'lily limp'.*

YELLOW FLAG

Iris, the rainbow goddess, has shed her alluring finery.
Like some parody of Rider Haggard's She, *the former beauty*
fades and shrivels to a husk. As the plump green
seed capsules dry out the tensions in their structure cause them
to writhe and split open in a gappy grin. The cracks reveal
the ripening seeds (roasted and drunk like coffee, they say)
which contain a promise of regeneration.
The Egyptians associated the iris with Osiris, god of the dead
and the afterlife, and the Greeks saw the flower as a symbol of life
and resurrection. These seeds will sprout new plants.

ASH

From suave, black-tipped twigs shapely with next year's growth,
ash keys hang in fat bunches that would impress a gaoler.
A year without keys was once thought to herald disaster: not just
the loss of a savoury snack (made by pickling the green
unripe ones), but something cosmic, like the death of a king.
But meanwhile use could be made of the pliable wood – chosen by
Cupid for his bows, and by many lesser mortals for their tools
and weapons. Young ash trees were cleft or holed to help cure
distemper, rickets, hernia, warts and (in Wales) impotence.
The growing tree evidently has mending properties: Yggdrasil, the
world tree which bound together heaven, hell and earth, was an ash.

RUGOSA ROSE

Sometime around 1066 (And All That) the Chinese were putting scented rugosa petals into pot-pourri. It arrived in the West from Japan towards the end of the eighteenth century and was called hedgehog rose or Rosa ferox *(the spines are fierce). We now call it* Rosa rugosa, *since its leaves are wrinkled and rugulose. One common name, Ramanas rose, seems to be a misreading of the Japanese* Hama-nasu *(an error forgivable in the circumstances, since Japan was closed to foreigners, and plant-hunters had to work heavily disguised).* Hama-nasu *means 'shore pear'. The rugosa rose certainly thrives by the seaside, but would not 'shore tomato' be more accurate?*

HOLM OAK

*Talk about confusing. The leathery leaves vary not only
from one tree to another, but even on the same plant.
Normally they are spiny and holly-like, so the tree was nicknamed
holly-oak (or holm-oak) when it arrived in Elizabethan England.
For a long time gardeners called it 'ilex' (confusing to us
today, since Ilex is the botanical name for holly). But they were
only displaying their classical credentials. It's native
to the Mediterranean; in fact, it's the original Roman ilex.*

*It makes a somewhat sombre evergreen, with long-lasting leaves.
Only when it perks up in June with golden catkins and new
silvery foliage did tree-lover Alan Mitchell think that the holm oak
stopped being 'unforgivably dull'.*

FIG

*This fig fruit has fed one of autumn's woozy supernumerary wasps.
A fitting irony, for figgy evolution has irrevocably entwined
plant and insect into mutual dependence for their convoluted sex-life.
It's a minute gall-wasp, actually, that quite incidentally effects
pollination by moving between male and female fig flowers in search
of that specialized, neuter gall-fig developed uniquely for her
benefit. When she finds one she lays her eggs there; inside they
hatch, mate and see to the survival of their species.*

*Fortunately today's cultivated female figs, liberated from all this
waspish business, ripen readily for our delight: but they are infertile.*

ACKNOWLEDGEMENTS

I would like to thank the following people: Penny David for her research, for bringing many of the wild fruits for the photographs from Wales, and for writing the descriptions of them with such wit and scholarship; Ray Watkins for her meticulous layout and design and her enthusiasm throughout; Thomas and Pepe Messel for hours spent searching for and finding wild fruit for the photographs; Graham Piggott for his professional and caring assistance; David Attenborough for his erudite and informative foreword; David Reynolds and Monica Macdonald at Bloomsbury for their help in publishing this small booklet.

Snowdon, 1997